CROSSROADS 2

Workbook

Marjorie Fuchs

with
Irene Frankel
Shirley Brod
of
Spring Institute for International Studies

Oxford University Press

Table of Contents

Cross-Reference to Crossroads 2 Student Book

Cross-Reference to Crossroads 2 Student Book

UNIT 1

Grammar

Level A

1. Match.

a. I am   she's

b. she is   he's

c. they are   I'm

d. it is   they're

e. we are   it's

f. you are   we're

g. he is   you're

2. Complete.

| her | his | ~~my~~ | our | their | your |

a. Hi. **My** name is Gloria.

b. _____ name is Van.

c. _____ name is Sue.

d. _____ teacher is Donna Jones.

e. Hi. What's _____ name?   _____ name is Ahmed.

f. _____ names are Pablo and Maria.

(Continued on page 2)

Grammar

Level A (continued)

---

3. Circle the answers.

Maria: Hi. ⬭I'm⬭ / She's Maria.

Van: Hello. My / His name is Van.

Maria: Where are you / are we from, Van?

Van: I'm / We're from Vietnam.

And this is my / your friend, Gloria.

He's / She's from El Salvador.

4. Complete and answer the questions. Use the information in 3.

am	are	is

a. __Is__ Van from Vietnam?

__Yes__, __he__ __is__ .

(Continued on page 3)

Grammar

b. _____ Gloria from Vietnam, too?

_____, _____ _____.

c. _____ Gloria and Van friends?

_____, _____ _____.

d. _____ YOU from Vietnam?

_____, _____ _____.

5. Complete. Have a conversation with Gloria.

_____: Hi. __My__ name is _____.
(Your name)

Gloria: Hi. _____ name is Gloria. _____ from El Salvador.

Where _____ you from?

_____: _____ from _____.
(Your name)

Gloria: _____ you a new student?

_____: _____, _____ _____.
(Your name)

Grammar   Level B

1. Write the contractions.

   a. you are   _you're_

   b. he is   _____

   c. we are   _____

   d. she is   _____

   e. they are   _____

   f. I am   _____

   g. it is   _____

2. Match.

a.	I	his
b.	you	her
c.	we	my
d.	she	their
e.	he	our
f.	they	its
g.	it	your

(a. I is connected by a line to my)

3. Complete.

a. _My_ name is Donna. _____ from the United States.

b. _____ name is Gloria. _____ from El Salvador.

c. _____ name is Ahmed. _____ from Afghanistan.

d. _____ name is Sue Le. And _____ name is Van Le. _____ from Vietnam.

e. _____ name is Pablo. And _____ name is Maria. _____ from Mexico.

(Continued on page 5)

Grammar   **Level B (continued)**

4. Ask and answer questions. Use the information in 3.

   a. Donna / the United States?

     <u>Is Donna from the United States?</u>

     <u>Yes, she is.</u>

   b. Gloria/the United States?

   c. Ahmed / Vietnam?

   d. Sue Le and Van Le / Korea?

   e. Pablo and Maria / Mexico?

   f. YOU / Mexico?

Writing   Level A

1. Read Van Le's story. Put in capital letters.

H
~~h~~is name is van le. he's

from vietnam. he's a student

at the westside community

adult school. his teacher is

donna jones. van's first

language is vietnamese. he

speaks a little english.

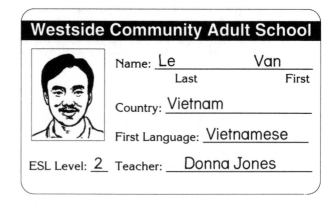

Westside Community Adult School

Name: Le   Van
       Last   First

Country: Vietnam

First Language: Vietnamese

ESL Level: 2 Teacher: Donna Jones

2. Read about Rosa. Write about her. Use Van Le's story in 1 as an example.

Her name is _____ Rosa Perez.

_____ Colombia.

_____

Oldbridge Adult School. _____

_____ Linda Ford.

_____ Spanish.

_____ a little English.

OLDBRIDGE ADULT SCHOOL

Name: Perez   Rosa
       Last   First

Country: Colombia

First Language: Spanish

Teacher: Linda Ford   ESL Level: 2

Writing

Level B

1. Read Van Le's story. Put in capital letters. Complete his ID card.

H
/his name is van le. he's

from vietnam. he's a student

at the westside community adult

school. his teacher is donna

jones. van's first language is

vietnamese. he speaks a little

english.

Westside Community Adult School

Name: _____
Last   First

Country: _____

First Language: _____

ESL Level: _2_ Teacher: _____

2. Read about Rosa. Write about her. Use Van Le's story in 1 as an example.

Her name is _____

_____

_____

_____

_____

_____

_____

OLDBRIDGE ADULT SCHOOL

Name: _Perez_   _Rosa_
Last   First

Country: _Colombia_

First Language: _Spanish_

Teacher: _Linda Ford_   ESL Level: _2_

Crossword Puzzle

Levels A and B

1. Complete the puzzle.

Across →

1. X

4. **I D Card**

6. 2345 First Avenue

10. I

11. (Hi !)

12. (Is that your husband?)
(Yes _____ name is Peter.)

13. (_____ to meet you.)

Down ↓

2. **Ahmed Jamali**

3.

4. (What ____ your name?)

5. (Where are you _____?)

7.

8. (How do you _____ it?)
(W-E-S-T-S-I-D-E)

9. **2**

UNIT 2

Game: Word Search

1. Find the words and circle them. The words go → and ↓.

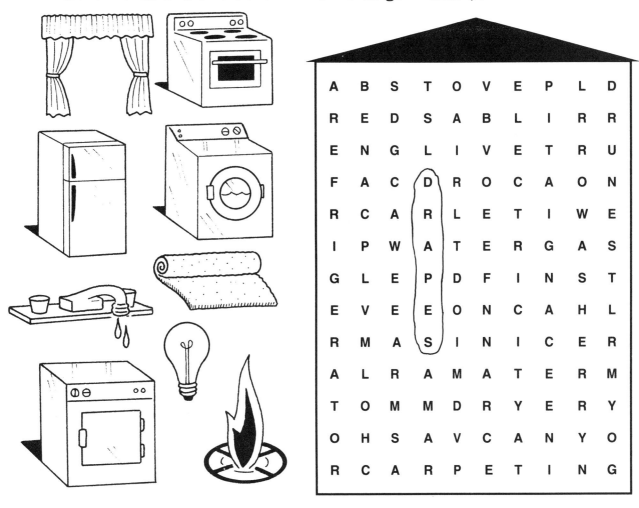

2. Put the words from 1 in appropriate rooms. You can use words twice.

Bedroom	Kitchen	Laundry Room
drapes		

Grammar

Level A

1. Look at Joe's new living room. Complete the sentences.

has	doesn't have

a. He __has__ a sofa, but he __doesn't have__ a chair.

b. He _____ a radio, but he _____ a TV.

c. He _____ drapes, but he _____ carpeting.

d. He _____ a lamp, but he _____ a table.

2. Look at Joe's shopping list. Complete the questions and answers.

chair
radio
table
drapes

a. (chair) __Does__ he need a chair?

___Yes, he does___

b. (radio) _____ a radio?

_____

c. (sofa) _____ ?

_____

d. (table) _____ ?

_____

e. (TV) _____ ?

_____

(Continued on page 11)

Grammar

Level A (continued)

3. **Look at Joe's new apartment. Complete the questions and answers.**

| Is there?
Are there? | Yes, there | is.
are. | No, there | isn't.
aren't. |

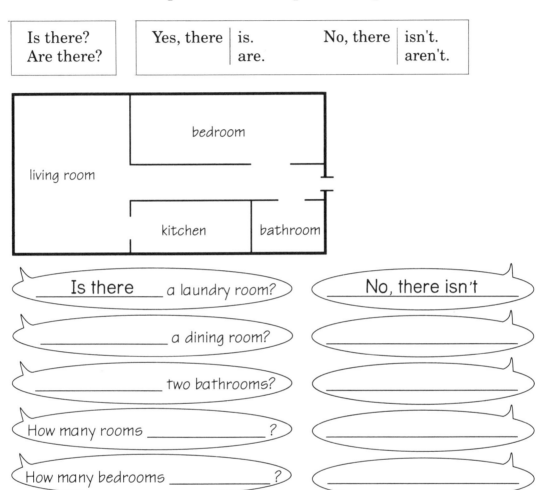

Is there _____ a laundry room?

No, there isn't

_____ a dining room?

_____

_____ two bathrooms?

_____

How many rooms _____ ?

_____

How many bedrooms _____ ?

_____

4. **Write about your house or apartment.**

a. My apartment/house has _____ , but it doesn't have

_____ .

b. I need _____ , but I don't need _____ .

c. There's a _____ in the kitchen.

d. There are _____ in the living room.

Grammar   Level B

1. Look at Joe's new living room. Write sentences.

| has   doesn't have |

a. a sofa/a chair

   He has a sofa, but he doesn't have a chair.

b. a radio/a TV

   _____

c. drapes/carpeting

   _____

d. a table/a lamp

   _____

2. Joe needs to go shopping for his new apartment. Complete his shopping list. Use the information in 1.

chair

(Continued on page 13)

Grammar

3. Look at the list in 2. Ask and answer questions.

a. (a chair) Does he need a chair _____?

   Yes, he does. _____

b. (a radio) _____?

   _____

c. (a sofa) _____?

   _____

d. (a table) _____?

   _____

e. (a TV) _____?

   _____

f. (carpeting) _____?

   _____

g. (drapes) _____?

   _____

h. (a lamp) _____?

   _____

(Continued on page 14)

Grammar

4. Look at Amy's neighborhood. Complete the conversation.

Is there a _____ ?	Yes, there is. No, there isn't.

Tom: How's your new neighborhood?

Amy: Oh, it's very nice.

Tom: _____Is there_____ a park near your apartment?

Amy: __No, there isn't.__

Tom: _____ a supermarket?

Amy: _____ . And there's a _____ across the street.

Tom: _____ a hospital?

Amy: _____ . But there's a _____ .

5. Write about Amy's neighborhood.

a. __There's a post office_____ across the street.

b. _____ two blocks away.

c. _____ on the corner.

d. _____ a block away.

Writing

1. Look at Amy's new apartment. Complete the description.

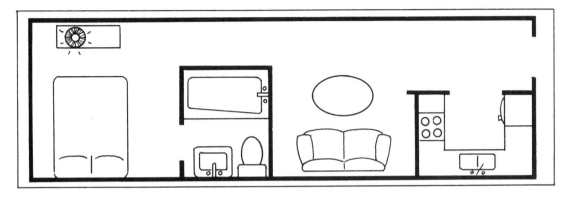

Amy has a new ____apartment____ . It has _____
a.   b.

rooms. There is a _____ , a _____ , and
c.   d.

a kitchen. The apartment has one _____ . Amy's apartment
e.

is furnished. There is a _____ and a table in the living room.
f.

The bedroom has a _____ and a dresser. There is a
g.

_____ on the dresser. It's a great apartment!
h.

2. Copy your description from 1. Use a separate piece of paper.

3. Look at Bill's new apartment. Write about it. Use 2 as an example. Use a separate piece of paper.

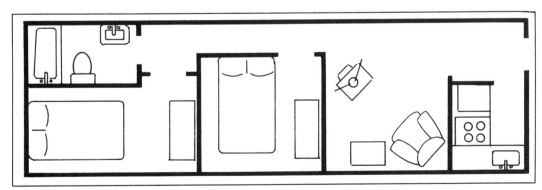

Writing

Level B

1. **Look at Amy's new apartment. Read the story. There are five mistakes in the story. Correct the mistakes.**

three

Amy has a new apartment. It has ~~two~~ rooms. There's a living room,

two bedrooms, and a kitchen. The apartment has one bathroom.

Amy's apartment is unfurnished. There is a sofa and a table in the

bedroom. The living room has a bed and dresser. It's a great apartment!

2. **Draw a floor plan of your dream apartment.**

3. **Describe your dream apartment. Use a separate piece of paper. Use 1 as an example.**

UNIT 3

Grammar

1. Complete.

a. print   _printed_____   b. sign   _____

c. use   _____   d. circle   _____

e. include   _____   f. check   _____

g. live   _____   h. study   _____

2. Look at the form.

Student Information Form   (Please print in ink.)

Mr. /Mrs. /Miss (Ms) Name: _Rosa Lopez_____
(Circle one.)
Address: _____3298 Third Avenue Apt. 5f_____
_____Bridgeton, CA_____

Marital status: single [   ]   married [✓]   separated [   ]
(Check one.)   divorced [   ]   widowed [   ]

Country of Origin: _____Mexico_____
Years of English: _____2_____

3. Complete the questions. Write the answers. Use the verbs in 1.

a. _Did___ she _print__ her name?   _No____ , _she didn't_____ .

b. _Did___ she _sign__ her name?   _Yes___ , _she did_____ .

c. _____ she _____ a pencil?   _____ , _____ .

d. _____ she _____ Ms.?   _____ , _____ .

e. _____ she _____ her ZIP Code?   _____ , _____ .

f. _____ she _____ single?   _____ , _____ .

g. _____ she _____ in Mexico?   _____ , _____ .

h. _____ she _____ English for 2 years?   _____ , _____ .

(Continued on page 18)

Grammar   Level A (continued)

4. **Write about Rosa. Use the information in 3.**

    a. She _____ didn't print _____ her name.

    b. She _____ signed _____ her name.

    c. She _____ a pencil.

    d. She _____ *Ms.*

    e. She _____ her ZIP Code.

    f. She _____ *single.*

    g. She _____ in Mexico.

    h. She _____ English for two years.

5. **Match**

a.	go	got
b.	buy	kept
c.	keep	went
d.	take	sent
e.	have	wrote
f.	get	bought
g.	send	took
h.	write	had

Grammar

1. Look at the form.

> ## Student Information Form   (Please print in ink.)
>
> Mr. /Mrs. /Miss (Ms.) Name: _Rosa Lopez_
> (Circle one.)
> Address: _3298 Third Avenue Apt. 5f_
> _Bridgeton, CA_
>
> Marital status: single [   ]   married [✓]   separated [   ]
> (Check one.)   divorced [   ]   widowed [   ]
>
> Country of Origin: _Mexico_
> Years of English: _2_

2. Ask questions about the form in 1.

a. print /sign name?

   Did she print her name or did she sign her name?

b. use a pen /pencil?

   _____

c. include apartment number /ZIP Code?

   _____

d. circle *Miss /Ms.?*

   _____

e. check *married /single?*

   _____

3. Answer the questions in 2.

a. _She didn't print her name. She signed her name._

b. _____

(Continued on page 20)

Grammar   Level B (continued)

c. _____

d. _____

e. _____

4. Complete the form. Use your own information.

Student Information Form (Please print in ink.)
Mr. /Mrs. /Miss /Ms. Name:_____
(Circle one.)
Address:_____
_____
_____
Marital status: single [   ]   married [   ]   separated [   ]
(Check one.)   divorced [   ]   widowed [   ]
Country of Origin:_____
Years of English: _____

5. Answer questions about your form.

a. Did you use a pencil?

    _____

b. Did you include your ZIP Code?

    _____

c. Did you check *single?*

    _____

d. Did you circle *Mr.?*

    _____

e. Did you study English in your country?

    _____

(Continued on page 21)

Grammar   Level B (continued)

6. **Complete.**

   a. go   <u>went</u>   b. buy   _____

   c. take _____   d. have _____

   e. get   _____   f. send _____

   g. write _____

7. **Complete the conversation. Use the correct form of the verb in parentheses ( ).**

   A: Hi, Victor. <u>Did</u> you <u>go</u> to the post office today?
   (go)

   B: Yes. I _____ this morning. I _____ to mail a letter
   (go)   (have)
   and buy a money order.

   A: _____ you _____ home?
   (do)   (write)

   B: No, I didn't. I _____ to Rosa.
   (write)

   A: Oh. Where is she now?

   B: In California. She _____ her first car last week.
   (buy)

   A: But Rosa doesn't drive!

   B: She drives now! She _____ the road test and _____ her
   (take)   (get)
   license last month.

   A: That's great!

   B: Yes. She's very happy. I _____ her a note of congratulations.
   (send)

Writing   Level A

1. **Write your name on the first line of this letter.**
   Read the letter. Put in capital letters.

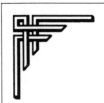

T
2510 /third avenue

columbus, ohio 43210

february 9, 1992

dear _____,
        (your name)

    hi. my name is carla rodriguez. i study english at
the downtown adult school. i'm in a level 2 class.

    i'm married and i have two children. my first
language is spanish. i'm 5'4", and i have black hair and
brown eyes.

    please write about yourself and send a picture.

                    sincerely,

                    carla

(Continued on page 23)

Writing

Level A (continued)

2. Complete this letter to Carla. Use your own information.

_____
(your address)

_____
(ZIP Code)

_____
(Date)

Dear Carla,

    Hi. My name _____. I study English at _____. I'm in a _____. My I'm _____. I'm first language _____. _____, and I _____.

    I'm sending you a picture.

    Please write again.

                      Sincerely,

                      _____
                      (your name)

3. Address this envelope to Carla. Write your return address.

29 USA

_____
_____
_____

_____
_____
_____

Writing   Level B

1. Write your name on the first line of this letter.
   Read the letter. Put in capital letters.

> T
> 2510 third avenue
> columbus, ohio 43210
> february 9, 1992
>
> dear _____,
>   (your name)
>   hi. my name is carla rodriguez. i'm a student in the united states.
> i'm studying english at the downtown adult school.
>   my teacher's name is mr. dennison. there are twenty students in my
> class. they're from five different countries, and they speak five different
> languages.
>   i'm from mexico, and my first language is spanish. i am 5'4", and i
> have black hair and brown eyes. i'm married and i have two children. we live
> in a furnished apartment. it's two blocks away from my school.
>   please write about yourself and send a picture.
>   sincerely,
>   carla

2. Write a letter to Carla. Use your own information. Use your own paper.
3. Address this envelope to Carla. Write your return address.

Game: Who is Pat Brown?   Levels A and B

1. **Cross out the item in each row that doesn't belong. Then write that item in the blank at the end of the correct row.**

a. 4'11"   5'2"   6'1"   ~~133~~   _____

b. black   hazel   red   blonde   _____

c. 1949   19061   1992   2001   _____

d. green   blue   brown   white   _____

e. 1940   19960   93207   11201   _____

f. 110   192   5'10"   200   _133_____

2. **Complete the application for an ID card. Use the information from the last column in 1.**

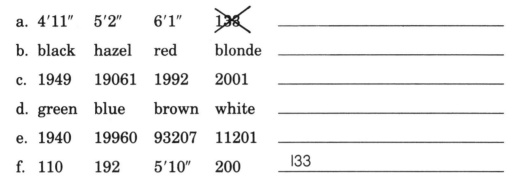

```
ID CARD

FULL NAME  Pat Brown                          ┌─────────┐
ADDRESS  5438 Fourth Street                   │         │
CITY  Media      STATE  PA  ZIP CODE_____     │    ?    │
SEX ( ) M  (✓) F                              │         │
COLOR HAIR _____  COLOR EYES _____      │         │
HEIGHT _____  WEIGHT  133  lbs.            └─────────┘
DATE OF BIRTH  6/11
```

3. **Choose the correct picture of Pat Brown. Use the information in 2.**

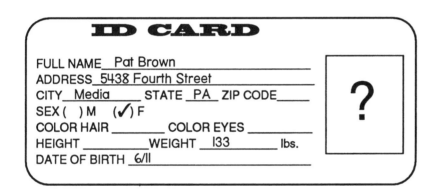

a.   b.   c.

d.   e.   f.

UNIT 4

Last Name: _____

School: _____

Grammar

Level A

1. Complete. | When   Where   How long |

A: _____ When _____ did he study English?
  a.
B: In 1990.

A: _____ did he study English?
  b.
B: In Taiwan.

A: _____ did he live there?
  c.
B: For twenty-one years.

A: _____ did he come to the United States?
  d.
B: In January.

2. Ask questions about Fran.

a. When/come to the U.S?

  ___ When did she come to the U.S. ___?

b. How long/study English?

  _____?

c. Where/study English?

  _____?

3. Answer the questions in 2. | for three years   in Italy   in 1988 |

a. ___ She came to the U.S. in 1988. ___

b. _____

c. _____

(Continued on page 27)

Grammar

4. Ask questions about Jim and Jean.

a. When/enroll in the adult school?

_____?

b. How long/go to the adult school?

_____?

c. Where/learn Spanish?

_____?

5. Answer the questions in 4.

in Mexico	for two years	three years ago

a. _____

b. _____

c. _____

Grammar

1. **Read the information about Andrea.**

> **School:**
> 1984 – 1988   Brookville High School, California
> 1988 – 1989   Brookville Cooking School, California
>   (studied cooking)
>
> **Work:**
> 1989 –1991   The Red Table Restaurant
>
> **Languages:**   Spanish (2 years, high school)
>   French (1 year, Brookville Adult School)

2. **Complete the interview with Andrea. Use the information in 1.**
   Use *Where*, *When*, and *How long*.

   Interviewer: Where did you _____ go to high school?
                                    a.

   Andrea: In California.

   Interviewer: _____ complete high school?
                                    b.

   Andrea: _____ .
                                    c.

   Interviewer: _____ study cooking?
                                    d.

   Andrea: At Brookville Cooking School.

   Interviewer: _____ study cooking?
                                    e.

   Andrea: For one year.

(Continued on page 29)

Grammar
Level B (continued)

Interviewer: Hhmmm. You worked at The Red Table Restaurant.

_____ work there?
f.

Andrea: For two years.

Interviewer: _____ study Spanish?
g.

Andrea: For _____ .
h.

Interviewer: _____ ?
i.

Andrea: At the Brookville Adult School.

3. Write about Andrea. Use the information from 2.

Andrea _____went_____ to school in California. She
a.

_____ high school in 1988. She _____
b.   c.

at the Brookville Cooking School for _____ .
d.

Then she _____ at the Red Table Restaurant for
e.

_____ .
f.

Andrea _____ Spanish for _____
g.   h.

in _____ , and she _____ French
i.   j.

at the _____ .
k.

Writing   **Level A**

1. Read about Fabio.

Fabio was born in Italy.

He studied English for

two years.

Fabio is married.

He has two children.

He came to the United States

three years ago.

2. Write about Carla.

___Carla was born_____ in Mexico.

_____

_____ three years.

_____ divorced.

_____ three children.

_____

_____ last year.

3. Write about Betty and Emily.

__Betty and Emily were born__

in Taiwan.

_____

for one year.

_____ single.

_____ no children.

_____ last year.

4. Write about yourself.

?
_____

I _____

_____

_____

_____

_____

_____

Writing

1. Read about this student. Complete his form.

Fabio Botero was born in Italy in 1948. He went to school there and studied English for two years.

Fabio is married and has two children. He came to the United States three years ago.

Enrollment Form

Mr./Mrs./Ms. Name: _____
  First   Last

Marital Status: Single [ ] Married [ ] Separated [ ]
      Divorced [ ] Widowed [ ]

Number of Children: _____

Date of Birth: __10/29/____   Birthplace: _____

Date of Arrival in U.S. 19____   Years of English Study ____

2. Write about Carla. Use 1 as an example.

Enrollment Form

Mr./Mrs./(Ms.)Name: __Carla__   __Gomez__
  First   Last

Marital Status: Single [ ]   Married [ ]   Separated [ ]
      Divorced [X]   Widowed [ ]

Number of Children: __3__

Date of Birth: __1/14/60__   Birthplace: __Mexico__

Date of Arrival in U.S. 19__91__   Years of English Study __3__

__Carla Gomez was born in Mexico in 1960.__

_____

_____

_____

_____

(Continued on page 32)

Writing

3. **Complete the form. Write about yourself.**

Enrollment Form

Mr./Mrs./Ms. Name: _____

                                First   Last

Marital Status: Single [   ]   Married [   ]   Separated [   ]

                      Divorced [   ]   Widowed [   ]

Number of Children: _____

Date of Birth: _____   Birthplace: _____

Date of Arrival in U.S. 19 ____   Years of English Study_____

_____

_____

_____

_____

_____

_____

Crossword Puzzle

Levels A and B

Across →

1. When <u>did</u> you come to the U.S.?
4. I'll meet you ____ school.
7. Not a.m.
8. A fire or accident
12. Not early
13. Your mother's brothers
15. Westside Community Adult ____
20. She came here three months ____.
21. ____ 1987
22. How long did you ____ English?

Down ↓

1. 10 cents
2. 2/24/92
3. Not married
5. He and she
6. She ____ to school for five years.
9. Mo.
10. Not difficult
11. ¢
14. You and me
16. ____ you speak English?
17. Fill ____ a form.
18. ____ I help you?
19. I studied English ____ two years.

Name: _____

Time: _____

Grammar

1. Complete the questions. Put a check (✓) in the correct box.

be	call	~~get~~	give	go		going to

                                                              Yes   No

a. _Is_ he __going to get__ the pain medicine?   ☐ ☑

b. _____ he _____ 911?   ☐ ☐

c. _____ they _____ to the hospital?   ☐ ☐

d. _____ the doctor _____ the woman cough syrup?   ☐ ☐

e. _____ she _____ OK?   ☐ ☐

(Continued on page 35)

Grammar   Level A (continued)

2. Write sentences. Use the information from 1.

going to   not going to

a. _He's not going to get_ _____ the pain medicine.

b. _____ 911.

c. _____ to the hospital.

d. _____ cough syrup.

e. _____ OK.

3. What about you? Answer the questions.

a. Are you going to see the doctor next week?

_____, _____ _____.

b. Are you going to go to the drugstore next week?

_____, _____ _____.

c. Are you going to take some medicine today?

_____, _____ _____.

4. Write sentences. Use the information in 3.

a. _I'm_ _____

b. _____

c. _____

Grammar

1. Complete the conversation.

be drive go ~~see~~ take	going to

A: __Is__ Alice ____going to see____ the doctor?
     a.   b.

B: Yes, _____.
               c.

A: _____ her brother _____ Alice there?
     d.   e.

B: No, _____. His car isn't working.
                   f.

    Alice _____ the bus with a friend.
               g.

A: When _____?
                     h.

B: In ten minutes.

A: _____ OK?
                   i.

B: Yes. Please don't worry.

2. The doctor gave these instructions. Read them and complete the sentences. Use *is going to* and *isn't going to*.

> **Dr. Burns • 1234 East Main Street • Bergandale CA**
>
>   August 11
>
> take 2 capsules every 4 hours for pain
> take aspirin for fever
> call Dr. Burns next week
> next appointment: September 11

(Continued on page 37)

Grammar

a. At 5:00 Alice _____is going to take_____ two capsules for pain.

   She __isn't going to take_____ three capsules.

b. At 6:00 Alice _____ more pain medicine.

   She _____ more medicine at 9:00.

c. Alice has a fever. She _____ antacid.

   She _____ aspirin.

d. Next week Alice _____ the doctor.

   She _____ 911.

e. On September 11, Alice _____ to the emergency

   room. She _____ the doctor at the clinic.

3. What about you? Complete and answer the questions.

going to

a. _____ you _____ to school tomorrow?

   _____, _____ _____.

b. _____ you _____ a friend tonight?

   _____, _____ _____.

c. _____ the doctor next week?

   _____, _____ _____.

d. _____ some medicine today?

   _____, _____ _____.

(Continued on page 38)

Grammar

Level B (continued)

4. **Write sentences. Use the information in 3.**

| going to | not going to |

a. _____

b. _____

c. _____

d. _____

Writing
Level A

1. Donna Walker went to the doctor. Read the doctor's instructions.

Dr. Ching Lin   342 Park Road, Lakeview, OH 45545 (216) 349-2839

stay home from school for a few days

take aspirin for fever

take medicine for cough

stay in bed

next appointment: Friday

2. Complete Mrs. Walker's letter to Donna's teacher.

> October 8
>
> Dear Mrs. Hardy,
>
> Donna has a _____ and a _____. She
> went _____ today. She has to _____
> for a few days.
> She has to take _____ and _____ in
> bed. She _____
> next Friday.
> I am sorry that Donna is going to miss school.
>
> Sincerely,
> Mrs. Walker

3. Copy the letter in 2. Use a separate piece of paper.

Writing

Level B

1. **Donna Walker went to the doctor. Read the doctor's instructions.**

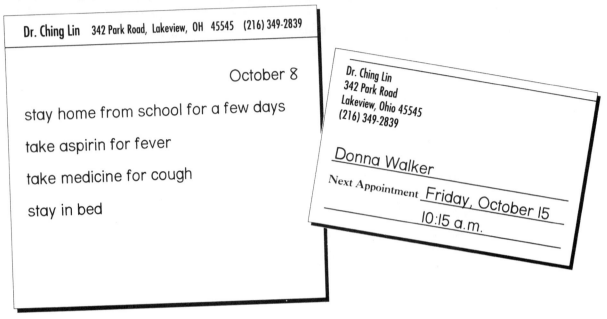

2. **Read Mrs. Walker's letter to Donna's teacher. There are five mistakes. Correct the mistakes.**

> October 8
>
> Dear Mrs. Hardy,
>
>   *cough*
>   Donna has a fever and a ~~stomachache~~. She went to the
> doctor yesterday. She has to stay home for a few months.
>
>   She has to take antacid, and stay in bed. She is going to see
> the doctor next Monday.
>
>   I am sorry that Donna is going to miss school.
>
>   Sincerely,
>   Mrs. Walker

(Continued on page 41)

Writing

3. **Write a letter about Tony. Use these notes and the corrected letter in 2 as an example.**

| Dr. Victor Santiago | 123 Sophia Street, Athens WA 98303 |

October 8

stay home for one week

take pain medicine for sprained ankle

rest

have X-ray Monday

October 8

Dear Mrs. Hardy,

_____

_____

_____

_____

_____

I am sorry _____

Sincerely,

_____
(Your name)

Game: "C" Search

1. Look at the picture. Write all the words that begin with *c*.

clinic _____   _____   _____

_____   _____   _____

_____   _____   _____

_____   _____   _____

_____   _____   _____

Name: _____

Date: _____

Grammar

Level A

1. Look at Tony's shopping list. What does he need?

some	not...any

Shopping List

onions	apples
bread	tea
potatoes	cookies

a. He needs some onions. _____

b. He doesn't need any tuna fish. _____

c. _____

d. _____

e. _____

f. _____

2. Ask and answer questions about Tony's shopping list in 1.

any...?	Yes, he does. No, he doesn't.

a. Does he need any bread _____?

   Yes, he does. _____

b. _____?

   _____

c. _____?

   _____

d. _____

   _____?

(Continued on page 44)

Grammar

3. Look at Mr. and Mrs. Wilson's kitchen shelf. Make statements.

not much		a lot of
not many		

a. <u>There's a lot of</u> _____ bread.

b. <u>There isn't much</u> _____ peanut butter.

c. _____ oil.

d. _____ cookies.

e. _____ tea.

4. Complete the conversation.

How much...? How many...?

A: <u>How many</u> _____ onions do you want?

B: <u>One bag</u> _____ , please.

A: And _____ oil do you need?

B: We need _____ .

A: What about bread? _____ bread do you need?

B: Oh, _____ . And _____ of cookies.

A: OK. And _____ peanut butter do you want?

B: _____ , please.

(Continued on page 45)

Grammar

5. Complete the conversation.

a lot of	much many

A: Does Sally drink ___much___ milk?

B: Yes, she does. She drinks ___a lot of___ milk.

A: Tommy doesn't drink _____ milk. He drinks

_____ apple juice, and he eats _____ rice.

I have to buy _____ rice every week.

B: Sally eats _____ potatoes. She doesn't eat _____ rice.

A: Does she eat _____ bananas?

B: No, she doesn't. But she eats _____ apples. She has an apple

every day.

6. Write about yourself. Use the foods in 3.

| drink
eat | a lot of | not...much
not...many | not...any |
|------|----------|-----------|----------|

a. __I__ _____ milk.

b. _____ apple juice.

c. _____ rice.

d. _____ potatoes.

e. _____ bananas.

f. _____ apples.

Grammar

Level B

1. **Look at Sue's shopping list. Ask and answer questions.**

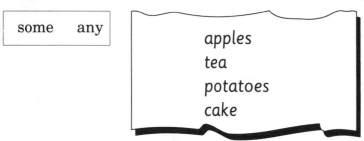

some	any

apples
tea
potatoes
cake

A: <u>Does she need any</u> _____ milk?

B: <u>She doesn't need any milk, but she needs some tea.</u> _____

A: _____ bananas?

B: _____

A: _____ ice cream?

B: _____

A: _____ onions?

B: _____

2. **Complete the conversation.**

much	many

a lot of

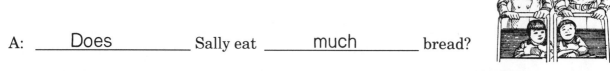

A: ___<u>Does</u>___ Sally eat ___<u>much</u>___ bread?

B: Yes, she does. She eats _____ bread. What about Tommy?

A: Tommy doesn't eat _____ bread, but he eats _____ rice.

_____ Sally drink _____ milk?

B: Oh, yes. She drinks _____ milk.

(Continued on page 47)

Grammar

Level B (continued)

A: Tommy doesn't drink _____ milk, but he drinks

_____ apple juice. And he eats _____ apples, too.

Do you buy _____ apples for Sally?

B: No. Sally doesn't eat _____ apples, but she eats

_____ bananas. She eats two bananas a day!

3. Write about yourself.

| not...much not...many | not...any | a lot of |

a. _____ bread.

b. _____ rice.

c. _____ tea.

d. _____ apple juice.

e. _____ apples.

f. _____ bananas.

g. _____.

h. _____.

(Continued on page 48)

Grammar

4. **Complete the conversation.**

| How much |
| How many |

A: _How many_ onions _____do_____ you want?

B: _One bag_____ , please.

A: And _____ oil _____ need?

B: We need _____ .

A: What about bread? _____ need?

B: Oh, _____ . And we need _____ of cookies, too.

A: OK. And _____ peanut butter _____ want?

B: _____ , please.

Writing   Level A

1. Look at Jane's shopping list. Complete the story.

Shopping List

1 lb. ground beef

2 lbs. potatoes

1 qt. orange juice

onions

let~~t~~uce

to~~m~~atoes

lb. = pound   qt. = quart
pkg. = package   doz. = dozen

Jane is going to go to the supermarket. She needs

a _____ pound of _____ ground beef,

_____ potatoes, and

_____ orange juice. Jane

also needs _____ onions,

but she doesn't need _____

lettuce or tomatoes.

2. Now look at Mark's shopping list. Write about Mark. Use Jane's story in 1 as an example.

Shopping List

1 doz. eggs

1 lb. cheese

tomatoes

1 pkg. cookies

c~~a~~ke

ic~~e~~cream

Mark is _____

_____

_____

_____

_____

_____

_____

_____

_____

Writing   **Level B**

1. **Look at Jane's shopping list and read the story. There are five mistakes in the story. Correct them.**

Shopping List

1 lb. ground beef

2 lbs. potatoes

1 qt. orange juice

onions

~~lettuce~~

~~tomatoes~~

Jane is going to go to the supermarket. She needs a
ground beef
pound of ~~chicken~~, three pounds of potatoes, and a

quart of milk. Jane also needs some tomatoes, but she

doesn't need any lettuce or onions.

2. **Look at the pictures. Complete Mark's shopping list.**

3. **Write about Mark. Use Jane's story in 1 as an example.**

Mark is _____

_____

_____

_____

_____

Game: Find the Food

Levels A and B

1. Look at the picture. Circle all the food.

2. Write the names of the food in 1.

onion _____   _____

_____   _____

_____   _____

_____   _____

Name: _____

S.S. #: _____

Grammar

Level A

1. Look at the picture. Complete the conversation.

was	wasn't
were	weren't

A: __Were__ Marta and Pedro in the U.S. in 1985?

B: __Yes__ , __they__ __were__ .

A: _____ Marta a cook?

B: _____ , _____ _____ . She _____ a _____ .

A: _____ Pedro a cashier, too?

B: _____ , _____ _____ . He _____ a delivery person.

A: _____ they happy with their jobs?

B: Marta _____ happy, but Pedro _____ very happy.

2. Write about yourself.

a. Were you in the United States in 1985?

_____ , _____ _____ .

b. Were you a student?

_____ , _____ _____ .

c. Were you employed?

_____ , _____ _____ .

d. Were you happy?

_____ , _____ _____ .

(Continued on page 53)

Grammar

Level A (continued)

3. **Marta is applying for a new job. Look at the list. Complete the conversation. Use _can_ and _can't_.**

	Yes	**No**
read and write English?	☑	[ ]
use a cash register?	☑	[ ]
work full-time?	[ ]	☑
work part-time?	☑	[ ]
work days?	[ ]	☑
work nights?	☑	[ ]
start immediately?	[ ]	☑
start next month?	☑	[ ]

a. __Can__ you __read__ and write English?   __Yes__, I __can__.

b. _____ _____ use a cash register?   _____, _____ _____.

c. _____ _____ work full-time?   _____, _____ _____.

d. _____ _____ _____ days?   _____, _____ _____.
But I _____ _____ nights.

e. OK. When can you start?
_____ _____ _____ immediately?   I _____ _____ next month.

(Continued on page 54)

Grammar

4. Complete this chart for yourself. Check (✓) the correct column

Can you...

		Yes	No
a.	speak English?	[ ]	[ ]
b.	speak another language?	[ ]	[ ]
c.	drive a car?	[ ]	[ ]
d.	drive a bus?	[ ]	[ ]
e.	use a sewing machine?	[ ]	[ ]
f.	cook?	[ ]	[ ]
g.	fix a car?	[ ]	[ ]

5. Write about yourself. Use the information in 4. Use *can* and *can't*.

a. _____

b. _____

c. _____

d. _____

e. _____

f. _____

g. _____

Grammar

1. Look at the information about Minh. Complete the interview.

> **Minh Lee**
> **102 Grove Street**
> **Bridgeton, CA**
> **93208**
>
> **Employment:**
>
> **1989-1990** Part-time cashier at ABC Drugstore
> Reason for leaving: laid off
>
> **Education:**
>
> **1988-1991** Full-time student at Bridgeton Community College

was
were

A: I see you worked at the ABC Drugstore, Mr. Lee.

_____Were_____ _____ a delivery person?

B: __No__ , ____I____ ____was____ a cashier.

A: _____ _____ a full-time job?

B: No, _____ _____. It _____ part-time.

I _____ a full-time student then.

A: I see. _____ _____ happy with your job at the drugstore?

B: Yes, _____ _____. I _____ very happy.

A: _____ they happy with you?

B: Yes, _____ _____.

A: Why did you leave?

B: The drugstore closed, and I _____ laid off.

(Continued on page 56)

Grammar

2. Carlos is speaking to a job counselor. Write the counselor's questions.

read? start? use? work? drive? fix?

a. __Can you use_____ a cash register?

b. _____ a car?

c. _____ English?

d. _____ a refrigerator?

e. _____ full-time?

f. _____ in the morning?

g. _____ a new job immediately?

3. Look at the information about Carlos. Answer the questions in 2.
Use *can* or *can't*.

Date available *next month*_____
Are you available   [ ] full-time   [✓] part-time?
What shifts can you work?   [✓] 7 a.m.–3 p.m. (first)
                            [✓] 3 p.m.–11 p.m. (second)
                            [ ] 11 p.m.–7 a.m. (third)
Languages: [✓] English   [ ] Spanish   [ ] other
Do you have a driver's license?   [✓] car   [ ] bus
Can you use these machines?   [ ] sewing machine   [✓] cash register
Can you fix machines?   [✓] TV   [ ] refrigerator   [ ] stove

a. __He can use a cash register,_____

   __but he can't use a sewing machine._____

(Continued on page 57)

Name: ______________________________

S.S. #: ______________________________

Grammar

Level B (continued)

b. ______________________________

____

c. ______________________________

____

d. ______________________________

____

e. ______________________________

____

f. ______________________________

____

g. ______________________________

____

Game: Job Search

Levels A and B

1. **Find the jobs that match the pictures. The words go → and ↓ .**

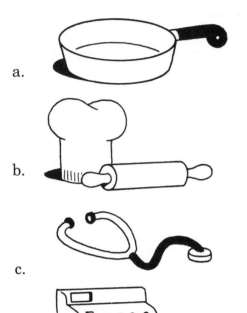

a.

b.

c.

d.

H	O	T	E	L	P	E	T	O	N	E	S	A	I	D
A	R	M	T	E	A	C	H	E	R	A	S	P	D	O
M	O	N	E	T	R	O	C	L	P	A	B	L	O	S
C	A	S	T	J	A	N	I	T	O	R	R	A	C	K
A	S	B	V	O	M	E	N	W	K	O	E	N	T	D
S	C	A	R	P	E	N	T	E	R	E	D	Y	O	U
H	A	K	E	E	D	I	M	S	U	M	C	A	R	E
I	C	E	A	T	I	M	A	G	O	G	E	T	O	N
E	M	R	I	L	C	O	O	K	F	O	O	D	I	T
R	O	N	L	H	M	V	K	R	N	W	T	Y	O	N

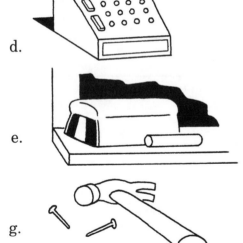

e.

g.

f.

h.

2. **Write the job titles.**

a. _____cook_____

b. _____

c. _____

d. _____

e. _____

f. _____

g. _____

h. _____

Writing

Level A

1. Look at the job notice. Read about the job. Complete the story.

HELP WANTED

Full-time hospital worker. $5.25/hr. 3:30p.m.–11:30p.m. No experience is necessary. Start now!

Oscar is going to apply for this job.

The notice is for a _____full_____-time

_____. No

_____ is necessary. The

job pays _____. It's for the

_____ shift, and it starts

_____.

2. Olga wants this job. Write about the job. Use 1 as an example.

PART-TIME

HELP NEEDED

Experienced cashier. $6.30/hr. 8:00 a.m.– 12:00 p.m. Start June 1.

Olga is _____

_____

_____

_____

_____

_____

_____

_____

Writing   Level B

1. Look at the job notice. Read about the job. There are four mistakes. Correct the mistakes.

Oscar is going to apply for this job.

The notice is for a ~~part~~- *full* time hospital

worker. No experience is necessary.

The job pays $5.75/hr. It's for the day

shift, and it starts next week.

2. Your friend wants a job. Write to him or her about this job notice. Look at the story in 1 for ideas.

HELP WANTED

Full-time/part-time cashiers. Start next month. All shifts. $6.24/hr. Experience not necessary, but preferred. Call for an interview.

_____
(today's date)

Dear _____,
(name of friend)

Hi. How are you? I know you are looking for a job. I saw a

job notice yesterday. The job is for a _____

_____

_____

_____

Is this a good job for you?

Good luck!   _____
(your name)

Grammar

1. Match.

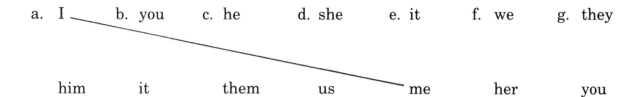

a. I   b. you   c. he   d. she   e. it   f. we   g. they

him   it   them   us   me   her   you

2. Complete. Use the words in 1.

I found ___it___ !
_____'s here.

a.

Did you see _____?
_____'re not here.

b.

Ask _____.
_____ knows.

c.

I asked _____.
_____ doesn't know.

d.

Don't ask _____.
_____ don't know.

e.

Call _____ tomorrow.
_____ need to know.

f.

Did Bill ask _____?
Do _____ know?

g.

(Continued on page 62)

Grammar

3. Where were these people last night? Write sentences.

| was   were | at home   at work   ~~at school~~   at the movies |

a.

Frank was at school. _____

b.

Gina and Tony _____

_____

c.

Sandy _____

_____

d.

Billy and Rick _____

_____

4. Complete the conversation. Use the information in 3.

| wasn't   was   weren't   were | | Where |

A: ___Was___ Frank at home last night?

B: ___No___, ___he___ ___wasn't.___ ___He___ ___was___

  ___at___ ___school___ .

A: _____ _____ Gina and Tony?

B: They _____ _____ _____ _____ .

A: _____ Billy and Rick at the movies, too?

(Continued on page 63)

Grammar

B: _____ , _____ _____.

A: Oh. _____ _____ they?

B: They _____ _____ _____.

A: _____ _____ Sandy?

B: _____ _____ _____ _____.

5. Complete the questions.

Where	What	When	Who	How		was	were

a. ___Where___ ___were___ you last night?

At school.

b. _____ _____ classmates _____ in school last week?

There were about thirty.

c. _____ _____ the first day of class?

It was on September 5.

d. _____ _____ your last teacher's name?

Linda Jones.

e. _____ _____ the first classmate you interviewed?

Sue Lee.

Grammar

1. Complete.

a. I   _____me_____   e. it   _____

b. you   _____   f. we   _____

c. he   _____   g. they   _____

d. she   _____

2. Complete the conversation. Use the words in 1.

Hi. Sue. How's your new job?
Do you like ___it__?

a.

_____It___'s OK! The workers are nice.
_____'re from Vietnam, too.

b.

That's nice. Do you speak
Vietnamese with _____?

c.

Yes. But I have to speak English with Mr.
Smith. _____'s American, and I can't speak
Vietnamese with _____. How's your job?

d.

I got laid off. I'm living with my sister now.
Do you know _____?

e.

No, I don't. What does _____ do?

f.

(Continued on page 65)

Grammar

Level B (continued)

_____'s a part-time cashier at a drugstore. Oh! It's late. _____ have to go now. Nice to see _____ again, Sue.

g.

Nice to see _____, too. Call _____ some time. _____ can go to a movie.

h.

3. **Complete the story about Sasha's grandmother and grandfather.**

| was   were |

My grandmother and grandfather _____were_____ born in Russia.
a.

They _____ married for fifty years and had five children. My
b.

mother _____ their second daughter.
c.

My grandfather _____ a mechanic, and my grandmother
d.

_____ a sewing machine operator. They _____ happy with
e.   f.

their jobs.

My grandmother died in 1990. She _____ eighty-two years
g.

old. My grandfather came to the United States in 1991. He _____
h.

happy in the Russia, but he isn't very happy now.

(Continued on page 66)

Grammar

4. Interview Sasha about his grandparents. Use the information in 3.

You: _____ Where was _____ your grandfather born?
                            a.

Sasha: In Russia.

You: _____ there, too?
                                  b.

Sasha: Yes, she was.

You: _____ your grandfather's job?
                       c.

Sasha: He was a mechanic, and my grandmother was a sewing

machine operator.

You: _____ happy with their jobs?
                       d.

Sasha: Yes, they were.

You: _____ married?
                       e.

Sasha: Fifty years.

You: When did your grandmother die?

Sasha: In 1990.

You: _____ then?
                   f.

Sasha: She was eighty-two.

You: And _____ ?
                       g.

Sasha: He was eighty-two, too.

Writing

Level A

1. Change the <u>underlined words</u> to the words in the box.

her	him	it	she	them

Hank,

Do you have the screwdriver? I need <u>the screwdriver</u>.
Bob doesn't have <u>the screwdriver</u>. I asked <u>Bob</u>. Anna
was here, too. I also asked <u>Anna</u>. <u>Anna</u> saw
<u>the screwdriver</u> yesterday. <u>The screwdriver</u> was on the
pegbboard next to the pliers. The pliers are there now.
I can see <u>the pliers</u> to the left of the hammer. But I
can't see the screwdriver. Please call me later.

Fred

2. Copy the new note.

Hank,

Do you have the screwdriver? I need it.

Bob

Writing

Level B

1. Complete Bill's note.

her	him	it	me	she

Hank,

Do you have the screwdriver? I need ___it___. Bob
                                      a.

doesn't have _____. I asked _____. Anna was here,
              b.   c.

too. I also asked _____. _____ saw _____
                    d.   e.   f.

yesterday. _____ was on the pegboard next to the
            g.

pliers. The pliers are there now. I can see _____ to
                                             h.

the left of the hammer. But I can't see the screwdriver.

Please call _____.
             i.

                              Fred

2. Rewrite the note. Change *the screwdriver* to *the scissors*.

Hank,

Do you have the scissors? I need them.

Bob

Game: Where are the nails?

1. Look at the picture. Circle all the nails.

2. Write the locations of the nails in 1.

in the wall

Name: _____

Hair Color: _____ Eye Color: _____

Grammar   Level A

1. Complete.

a. small _____   smaller _____

b. big _____   bigger _____

c. short _____   _____

d. _____   fatter _____

e. old _____   _____

f. long _____   _____

g. _____   thinner _____

h. young _____   _____

i. tall _____   _____

2. Look at the pictures of Mary and Ann. Read the sentences. Put a check (✓) in the correct box.

Mary   Ann

		Yes	No
a.	Mary is taller than Ann.	☐	☐
b.	Ann is shorter than Mary.	☐	☐
c.	Ann is younger than Mary.	☐	☐
d.	Mary's sweater is smaller than Ann's sweater.	☐	☐
e.	Ann's hair is shorter than Mary's hair.	☐	☐
f.	Ann's skirt is longer than Mary's skirt.	☐	☐

(Continued on page 71)

Grammar

Level A (continued)

3. **Look at the pictures of Lee and Rob. Write sentences about them. Use <u>one</u> of the words in parentheses ( ).**

a. Lee <u>is older than</u> _____ Rob.   (old / young)

b. _____ than Lee.   (fat / thin)

c. _____ than Rob.   (tall / short)

d. Lee's hair _____ Rob's hair.   (long / short)

e. Lee's jacket _____ .   (small / big)

Grammar

1. Complete.

a. small   <u>smaller</u>   b. big   _____

c. long   _____   d. short   _____

e. old   _____   f. thin   _____

g. fat   _____   h. young   _____

i. tall   _____

2. Look at the pictures of Mary and Ann. Read the sentences. Write *Yes, that's right.* or *No, that's wrong.* Correct the sentences that are wrong.

Mary   Ann

a. Mary is <u>older</u> than Ann.

   <u>No, that's wrong. Mary is younger than Ann.</u>

b. Ann is <u>shorter</u> than Mary.

_____

c. Mary is <u>thinner</u> than Ann.

_____

d. Mary's hair is <u>longer</u> than Ann's hair.

_____

(Continued on page 73)

Grammar

Level B (continued)

e. Ann's sweater is <u>bigger</u> than Mary's sweater.

_____

f. Ann's sweater is <u>shorter</u> than Mary's sweater.

_____

g. Mary's skirt is <u>longer</u> than Ann's skirt.

_____

3. These people are in the store. Complete the conversations.

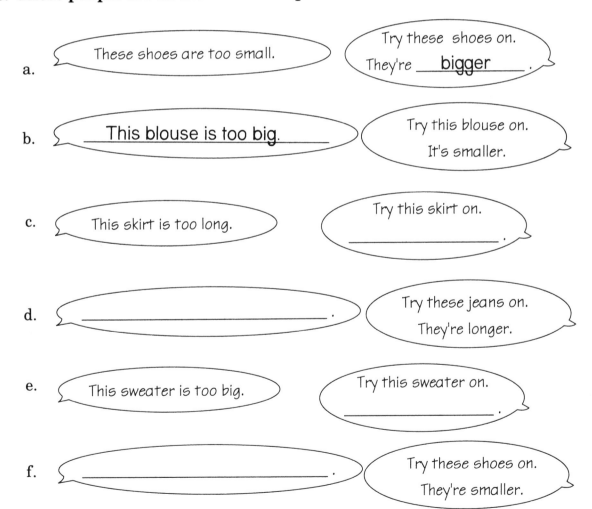

a. These shoes are too small.
Try these shoes on. They're ___**bigger**___.

b. ___This blouse is too big.___
Try this blouse on. It's smaller.

c. This skirt is too long.
Try this skirt on. _____.

d. _____.
Try these jeans on. They're longer.

e. This sweater is too big.
Try this sweater on. _____.

f. _____.
Try these shoes on. They're smaller.

Writing   Level A

1. Look at the receipt. Read the thank you note. Complete the note.

```
********************
LACY'S  DEPARTMENT  STORE

DATE: JUNE 11

1 WOMAN'S SWEATER    $25.00
2 BLOUSES @ $21.50   $43.00
5 PR. SOCKS @ $3.25  $16.25
---------------------------
SUBTOTAL             $84.25
TAX                  $ 5.05

TOTAL                $89.30
********************
```

                                                    June 11

Dear Aunt Sally,

        Thank you for the birthday money. _Today_ I went
                                              a.
shopping at Lacy's Department _____. I bought a lot
                                    b.
of clothes. I bought a blue _____, _____ white
                                  c.   d.
blouses, and some _____. Now I have clothes for my
                        e.
new job!

        Thanks again!

                                              Brenda

(Continued on page 75)

Writing

2. **Look at the receipt. Write a thank you note to a friend or relative. Use the note in 1 as an example.**

```
******************************

ROBINSON'S DEPARTMENT STORE

DATE 11/11

2 PR. JEANS @ 32.00          $64.00
1 PR. SHOES                  $26.00
1 SWEATER                    $34.00

                  SUBTOTAL  $124.00
                       TAX  $   7.44
                     TOTAL  $131.44

****************************
```

November 11

Dear _____ ,

Thank you for the birthday money.
_____ I _____ _____ at Robinson's
_____ _____. _____
_____ a lot of clothes. I bought some
jeans, _____ shoes, and a
_____. Now I have clothes for
_____.

Thanks again!

_____

Writing   Level B

1. **Look at the receipt. Read the thank you note. Correct the note.**

```
************************
LACY'S DEPARTMENT STORE

DATE: JUNE 11

1 WOMAN'S SWEATER   $25.00
2 BLOUSES @ $21.50  $43.00
5 PR. SOCKS @ $3.25 $16.25
- - - - - - - - - - - - - -
SUBTOTAL            $84.25
TAX                 $ 5.05

TOTAL               $89.30
************************
```

June 12

Dear Aunt Sally,

                                    Yesterday

     Thank you for the birthday money. ~~Today~~ I

went shopping at Robinson's Department Store. I

bought a lot of tools. I bought a skirt, three blouses,

and five pairs of shoes. Now I have clothes for my

new job.

     Thanks again!

                                     Brenda

(Continued on page 77)

Writing

2. **Look at the clothes. Complete the store receipt.**

```
*************************
R & S  D E P A R T M E N T  S T O R E
*************************
D A T E  11/11

ITEM                    PRICE
.................................
.................................
.................................
.................................
            SUBTOTAL
                 TAX
               TOTAL
.................................
```

3. **Write a thank you note to a friend or relative. Use the information in 2.
   Use the note in 1 as an example.**

November 11

Thank You

Game: Word Search

Levels A and B

1. There are ten clothing words in the suitcase. The words go

   and ↓ . Find the words and circle them.

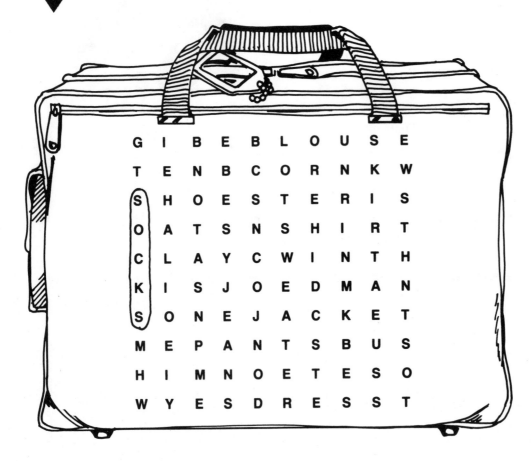

```
G   I   B   E   B   L   O   U   S   E
T   E   N   B   C   O   R   N   K   W
S   H   O   E   S   T   E   R   I   S
O   A   T   S   N   S   H   I   R   T
C   L   A   Y   C   W   I   N   T   H
K   I   S   J   O   E   D   M   A   N
S   O   N   E   J   A   C   K   E   T
M   E   P   A   N   T   S   B   U   S
H   I   M   N   O   E   T   E   S   O
W   Y   E   S   D   R   E   S   S   T
```

2. Write the words in 1.

   socks

   _____   _____

   _____   _____

   _____   _____

   _____   _____

Grammar

Level A

1. Complete the questions.

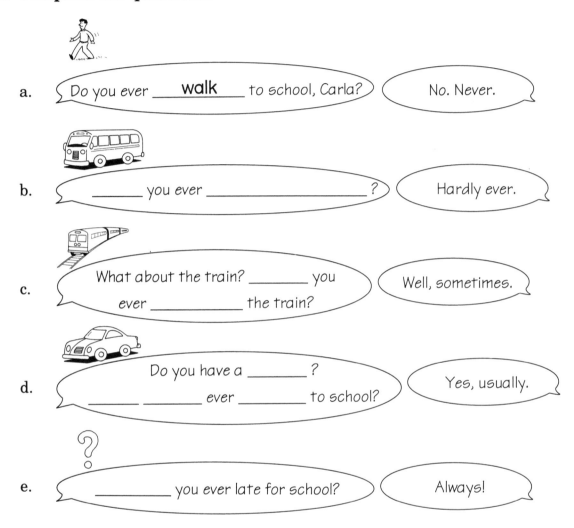

a. Do you ever _____**walk**_____ to school, Carla?   No. Never.

b. _____ you ever _____ ?   Hardly ever.

c. What about the train? _____ you ever _____ the train?   Well, sometimes.

d. Do you have a _____ ? _____ _____ ever _____ to school?   Yes, usually.

e. _____ you ever late for school?   Always!

2. Write about Carla. Use the information in 1.

a. _She never walks to school._____

b. _____

c. _____

d. _____

e. _____

Grammar

Level B

1. Complete the conversation.

Ann: Do you _____ ever _____ walk to school?
　　　　　　　　　　a.

Ben: No. I _____ walk to school.
　　　　　　　　　b.

Ann: _____ you _____ _____ the train?
　　　　　　　c.　　　　　　　　d.　　　　　　　e.

Ben: Sometimes. But I usually _____ the bus.
　　　　　　　　　　　　　　　　　　　f.

Ann: _____ _____ is the trip?
　　　　　g.　　　　　h.

Ben: It's usually about twenty minutes.

Ann: _____ _____ is it?
　　　　　i.　　　　　j.

Ben: $1.25.

Ann: _____ you _____ late for school?
　　　　　k.　　　　　　　l.

Ben: Yes, sometimes.

2. Write about Ben. Use the information in 1.

a. He never walks to school. _____

b. _____ ,

　　but he _____

c. _____

d. _____

e. _____

(Continued on page 81)

Grammar

**3. Complete the charts. Put a check (✓) in the correct column.
Use your own information.**

How do you get to school?

a.

b.

c.

d.

	always	usually	sometimes	hardly ever	never
a.					
b.					
c.					
d.					
e.					

e. Are you ever late for school?

4. Write about yourself. Use the information in 3.

a. _____

b. _____

c. _____

d. _____

e. _____

Writing   Level A

1. Correct Dan's letter. Add these words:

sentence (6)   always
sentence (7)   usually
sentence (8)   usually
sentence (9)   hardly ever
sentence (10)   sometimes
sentence (13)   always

December 21

Dear Helen,

    Hi. How are you? Do you remember my brother
    1   2   3

Ken? You met him last year. He moved in November from
                    4   5
                                              always

Yorktown, and now he lives near you in Portsmouth. I ˄visit

him in January. I take the train to Yorktown, but this time
    6   7

I'm going to drive to Portsmouth. The trip is about two
                                                    8

hours. I arrive late. Ken has to work, and I have some free
        9   10

time. Are you going to be home on January 17? I can drive
                            11   12

to your house. It's nice to see you!
                    13

    Please write soon.
        14

                              Dan

---

2. Copy the corrected letter in 1. Use a separate piece of paper.

Writing   Level B

1. **Correct Anna's letter. Put in capital letters. Add these words:**

sentence (5)   always

sentence (6)   usually

sentence (8)   usually

sentence (9)   sometimes

sentence (10)   usually

sentence (11)   hardly ever

sentence (12)   usually

sentence (14)   always

                                   A
                                April 6

  D   K
dear Kim,

       how are you? i think about you a lot. today i
          1   2

bought a plane ticket to allentown. i'm going to visit
     3   **always**   4

my brother. i visit him in april. the ticket costs
           ^   5   6

about $300. this time there was a special fare, and it
                           7

was only $250. the trip takes three hours.
                8

       my brother meets me at the airport, but this time
                  9

i'm going to rent a car. the trip from the aiport to my
                       10

brother's apartment takes an hour. we are late.
                     11

       i stay in allentown for a week, but this time i'm
             12

going to be there for about a month. can we meet one
                       13

weekend? it's nice to see you!
          14

       Please write.
         15

                                 anna

---

2. **Copy the corrected letter in 1. Use a separate piece of paper.**

Game: "T" Search

1. Look at the picture. Write all the words that begin with *t*.

television _____ _____

_____ _____ _____

_____ _____ _____

_____ _____ _____

_____ _____ _____

Answer Key

UNIT 1

Grammar Level A

Exercise 1
a. I'm b. she's c. they're d. it's e. we're f. you're
g. he's

Exercise 2
a. My b. His c. Her d. Our e. your, My f. Their

Exercise 3
a. I'm b. My c. are you d. I'm e. my f. She's

Exercise 4
a. Is, Yes, he is.
b. Is, No, she isn't.
c. Are, Yes, they are.
d. Are, (Answers will vary.)

Exercise 5
(Answers will vary.)

Grammar Level B

Exercise 1
a. you're b. he's c. we're d. she's e. they're f. I'm
g. it's

Exercise 2
a. my b. your c. our d. her e. his f. their g. its

Exercise 3
a. My, I'm b. Her, She's c. His, He's
d. Her, his, They're e. My, my, We're

Exercise 4
a. Is Donna from the United States?
   Yes, she is.
b. Is Gloria from the United States?
   No, she isn't.
c. Is Ahmed from Vietnam?
   No, he isn't.
d. Are Sue Le and Van Le from Korea?
   No, they're not.
e. Are Pablo and Maria from Mexico?
   Yes, they are.
f. Are you from Mexico?
   (Answers will vary.)

Writing Level A

Exercise 1
His name is Van Le. He's from Vietnam. He's a student at the Westside Community Adult School. His teacher is Donna Jones. Van's first language is Vietnamese. He speaks a little English.

Exercise 2
Her name is Rosa Perez. She's from Colombia. She's a student at the Oldbridge Adult School. Her teacher is Linda Ford. Rosa's first language is Spanish. She speaks a little English.

Writing Level B

Exercise 1
(See Writing Level A, Exercise 1)
Last Name: Le

First Name: Van
Country: Vietnam
First Language: Vietnamese
ESL Level: 2
Teacher: Donna Jones

Exercise 2
(See Writing Level A, Exercise 2)

Crossword Puzzle Levels A and B

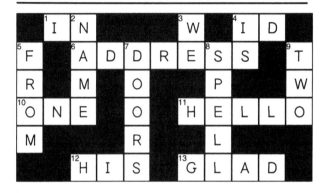

UNIT 2

Game: Word Search Levels A and B

Exercise 1

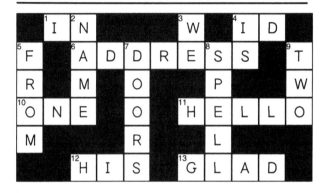

Exercise 2
(Answers may vary.)

Bedroom: drapes, carpeting, electricity
Kitchen: gas, refrigerator, electricity, stove, water
Laundry Room: dryer, electricity, water, washer

Grammar Level A

Exercise 1
a. has...doesn't have
b. doesn't have...has

c. doesn't have...has
d. has...doesn't have

Exercise 2
a. Does	Yes, he does.
b. Does he need	Yes, he does.
c. Does he need a sofa?	No, he doesn't.
d. Does he need a table?	Yes, he does.
e. Does he need a TV?	No, he doesn't.

Exercise 3
a. Is there	No, there isn't.
b. Is there	No, there isn't.
c. Are there	No, there aren't.
d. are there	Three.
e. are there	One.

Exercise 4
(Answers will vary.)

Grammar Level B

Exercise 1
a. He has a sofa, but he doesn't have a chair.
b. He doesn't have a radio, but he has a TV.
c. He doesn't have drapes, but he has carpeting.
d. He doesn't have a table, but he has a lamp.

Exercise 2
Shopping List: chair, radio, drapes, table

Exercise 3
a. Does he need a chair?	Yes, he does.
b. Does he need a radio?	Yes, he does.
c. Does he need a sofa?	No, he doesn't.
d. Does he need a table?	Yes, he does.
e. Does he need a TV?	No, he doesn't.
f. Does he need carpeting?	No, he doesn't.
g. Does he need drapes?	Yes, he does.
h. Does he need a lamp?	No, he doesn't.

Exercise 4
A: How's your new neighborhood?
B: Oh, it's very nice.
A: Is there a park near your apartment?
B: No, there isn't.
A: Is there a supermarket?
B: Yes, there is. And there's a post office across the street.
A: Is there a hospital?
B: No, there isn't. But there's a clinic.

Exercise 5
a. There is a post office across the street.
b. There is a clinic two blocks away.
c. There is a drugstore on the corner.
d. There is a supermarket a block away.

Writing Level A

Exercise 1
(Order may vary.)
a. apartment   b. three   c. living room   d. bedroom
e. bathroom   f. sofa   g. bed   h. lamp

Exercise 2
Amy has a new apartment. It has three rooms. There's a living room, a bedroom, and a kitchen. The apartment has one bathroom. Amy's apartment is furnished. There is a sofa and table in the living room. The bedroom has a bed and dresser. There is a lamp on the dresser. It's a great apartment!

Exercise 3
Bill has a new apartment. It has four rooms. There's a living room, two bedrooms, and a kitchen. The apartment has one bathroom. Bill's apartment is furnished. There is an armchair, table, and TV in the living room. The bedrooms have beds and dressers. It's a great apartment!

Writing Level B

Exercise 1

Mistakes: It has three rooms, not two rooms. There is one bedroom, not two bedrooms. It is furnished, not unfurnished. The sofa and table are in the living room, not the bedroom. The bedroom, not the living room, has a bed and dresser.

Exercises 2 and 3
(Answers will vary.)

UNIT 3

Grammar Level A

Exercise 1
a. printed   b. signed   c. used   d. circled
e. included   f. checked   g. lived   h. studied

Exercise 3
a. Did...print	No, she didn't.
b. Did...sign	Yes, she did.
c. Did...use	No, she didn't.
d. Did...circle	Yes, she did.
e. Did...include	No, she didn't.
f. Did...check	No, she didn't.
g. Did...live	Yes, she did.
h. Did...study	Yes, she did.

Exercise 4
a. She didn't print her name.
b. She signed her name.
c. She didn't use a pencil.
d. She circled *Ms.*
e. She didn't include her ZIP code.
f. She didn't check *single*.
g. She lived in Mexico.
h. She studied English for two years.

Exercise 5
a. went   b. bought   c. kept   d. took
e. had   f. got   g. sent   h. wrote

Grammar Level B

Exercise 2
a. Did she print her name or did she sign her name?
b. Did she use a pen or did she use a pencil?
c. Did she include her apartment number or did she include her ZIP Code?
d. Did she circle *Miss* or did she circle *Ms.?*
e. Did she check *married* or did she check *single?*

Exercise 3
a. She didn't print her name. She signed her name.
b. She used a pen. She didn't use a pencil.
c. She included her apartment number. She didn't include her ZIP Code.

d. She didn't circle *Miss*. She circled *Ms.*

e. She checked *married*. She didn't check *single*.

Exercise 4 and 5
(Answers will vary.)

Exercise 6
a. went   b. bought   c. took   d. had   e. got
f. sent   g. wrote

Exercise 7
A: Hi, Victor. Did you go to the post office today?

B: Yes. I went this morning. I had to mail a letter and buy a money order.

A: Did you write home?

B: No, I didn't. I wrote to Rosa.

A: Oh. Where is she now?

B: In California. She bought her first car last week.

A: But Rosa doesn't drive!

B: She drives now! She took the road test and got her license last month.

A: That's great!

B: Yes. She's very happy. I sent her a note of congratulations.

Writing Level A

Exercise 1

                                   2510 Third Avenue
                                   Columbus, Ohio 43210
                                   February 9, 1992

Dear _____ ,
    (your name)

Hi. My name is Carla Rodriguez. I study English at the Downtown Adult School. I'm in a Level 2 class.

I'm married and I have two children. My first language is Spanish. I'm 5' 4", and I have black hair and brown eyes.

Please write about yourself and send a picture.

                                   Sincerely,
                                   Carla

Exercises 2 and 3
(Answers will vary.)

Writing Level B

Exercise 1

                                   2510 Third Avenue
                                   Columbus, Ohio 43210
                                   February 9, 1992

Dear _____ ,
    (your name)

Hi. My name is Carla Rodriguez. I'm a student in the United States. I'm studying English at the Downtown Adult School.

My teacher's name is Mr. Dennison. There are twenty students in my class. They're from five different countries, and they speak five different languages.

I'm from Mexico, and my first language is Spanish. I am 5' 4", and I have black hair and brown eyes. I'm married and I have two children. We live in a furnished apartment. It's two blocks away from my school.

Please write about yourself and send a picture.

                                   Sincerely,
                                   Carla

Exercises 2 and 3
(Answers will vary.)

Game: Who is Pat Brown? Levels A and B

Exercise 1
The order of the misplaced items is: a. 5'10", b. white, c. 1940, d. hazel, e. 19061, f. 133.

Exercise 2
FULL NAME Pat Brown
ADDRESS 5438 Fourth Street
CITY Media   STATE PA   ZIP CODE   19061
SEX [F]   COLOR HAIR White   COLOR EYES   Hazel
HEIGHT 5'10"   WEIGHT 133 lbs.
DATE OF BIRTH June 11, 1940

Exercise 3
Pat Brown's picture is **e**.

UNIT 4

Grammar Level A

Exercise 1
a. When   b. Where   c. How long   d. When

Exercise 2
a. When did she come to the U.S.?
b. How long did she study English?
c. Where did she study English?

Exercise 3
a. She came to the U.S. in 1988.
b. She studied English for three years.
c. She studied English in Italy.

Exercise 4
a. When did they enroll in the adult school?
b. How long did they go to the adult school?
c. Where did they learn Spanish?

Exercise 5
a. They enrolled in the adult school three years ago.
b. They went to the adult school for two years.
c. They learned Spanish in Mexico.

Grammar Level B

Exercise 2
a. Where did you go to high school?
b. When did you complete high school?
c. I completed high school in 1988./In 1988.
d. Where did you study cooking?
e. How long did you study cooking?
f. How long did you work there?
g. How long did you study Spanish?
h. For two years.
i. Where did you study French?

Exercise 3
Andrea went to school in California. She completed high school in 1988. She studied cooking at the Brookville Cooking School for one year. Then she worked at the Red Table Restaurant for two years.

Andrea studied Spanish for two years in high school, and she studied French at the Brookville Adult School.

Writing Level A

Exercise 2
Carla was born in Mexico.
She studied English for three years.
Carla is divorced. She has three children.
She came to the United States last year.

Exercise 3
Betty and Emily were born in Taiwan.
They studied English for one year.
Betty and Emily are single. They have no children.
They came to the United States last year.

Exercise 4
(Answers will vary.)

Writing Level B

Exercise 1
Name: Mr. Fabio Botero
Marital Status: Married
Number of Children: 2
Date of Birth: 1948
Birthplace: Italy
Date of Arrival in U.S.: (Answers will vary.)
Years of English Study: 2

Exercise 2
Carla Gomez was born in Mexico in 1960.
She went to school there and studied English
for three years. Carla is divorced and has three children.
She came to the United States _____ years ago.
(Answer will vary.)

Exercise 3
(Answers will vary.)

Crossword Puzzle Levels A and B

UNIT 5

Grammar Level A

Exercise 1

a.	Is…going to get	No
b.	Is…going to call	No
c.	Are…going to go	Yes
d.	Is…going to give	No
e.	Is…going to be	Yes

Exercise 2
a. He's not going to get the pain medicine.
b. He's not going to call 911.
c. They are going to go to the hospital.
d. The doctor's not going to give the woman
   cough syrup.
e. She is going to be OK.

Exercises 3 and 4
(Answers will vary.)

Grammar Level B

Exercise 1
A: Is Alice going to see the doctor?
B: Yes, she is.
A: Is her brother going to drive Alice there?
B: No, he isn't. His car isn't working.
   Alice is going to take the bus with a friend.
A: When are they going to go?
B: In ten minutes.
A: Is she going to be OK?
B: Yes. Please don't worry.

Exercise 2
a. is going to take…isn't going to take
b. isn't going to take…is going to take
c. isn't going to take…is going to take
d. is going to call…isn't going to call
e. isn't going to go…is going to see

Exercises 3 and 4
(Answers will vary.)

Writing Level A

Exercise 3
Donna has a fever and a cough. She went to the doctor
today. She has to stay home from school for a few days.
She has to take cough medicine and stay in bed. She is
going to see the doctor next Friday. I am sorry that Donna
is going to miss school.

Writing Level B

Exercise 2
a stomachache → a cough
yesterday → today
months → days
antacid → cough medicine/aspirin
Monday → Friday

Exercise 3
Dear Mrs. Hardy,
Tony has a sprained ankle. He went to the doctor today.
He has to stay home from school for one week. He has to
take pain medicine and rest. He is going to have an X-ray
on Monday. I am sorry that Tony is going to miss school.
Sincerely,
(your name)

clinic, clock, check, chalk, chalkboard, child, cast, chair, car, cough, cough syrup, carpeting, capsules, cat

UNIT 6

Grammar Level A

Exercise 1
a. He needs some onions.
b. He doesn't need any tuna fish.
c. He needs some apples.
d. He needs some potatoes.
e. He needs some tea.
f. He doesn't need any cake.

Exercise 2
a. Does he need any bread?
   Yes, he does.
b. Does he need any bananas?
   No, he doesn't.
c. Does he need any ice cream?
   No, he doesn't.
d. Does he need any cookies?
   Yes, he does.

Exercise 3
a. There's a lot of bread.
b. There isn't much peanut butter.
c. There isn't much oil.
d. There are a lot of cookies.
e. There's a lot of tea.

Exercise 4
A: How many onions do you want?
B: One bag, please.
A: And how much oil do you need?
B: We need a/one bottle.
A: What about bread? How much bread do you need?
B: Oh, two loaves. And a package of cookies, too.
A: OK. And how much peanut butter do you want?
B: Three jars, please.

Exercise 5
A: Does Sally drink much milk?
B: Yes, she does. She drinks a lot of milk.
A: Tommy doesn't drink much milk. He drinks a lot of apple juice, and he eats a lot of rice. I have to buy a lot of rice every week.
B: Sally eats a lot of potatoes. She doesn't eat much rice.
A: Does she eat many bananas?
B: No, she doesn't. But she eats a lot of apples. She has an apple every day.

Exercise 6
(Answers will vary.)

Grammar Level B

Exercise 1
A: Does she need any milk?
B: She doesn't need any milk, but she needs some tea.
A: Does she need any bananas?
B: She doesn't need any bananas, but she needs some apples.
A: Does she need any ice cream?

B: She doesn't need any ice cream, but she needs some cake.
A: Does she need any onions?
B: She doesn't need any onions, but she needs some potatoes.

Exercise 2
A: Does Sally eat much bread?
B: Yes, she does. She eats a lot of bread. What about Tommy?
A: Tommy doesn't eat much bread, but he eats a lot of rice. Does Sally drink much milk?
B: Oh, yes. She drinks a lot of milk.
A: Tommy doesn't drink much milk, but he drinks a lot of apple juice. And he eats a lot of apples, too. Do you buy many apples for Sally?
B: No. Sally doesn't eat many apples, but she eats a lot of bananas. She eats two bananas a day!

Exercise 3
(Answers will vary.)

Exercise 4
(See Grammar Level A, Exercise 4.)

Writing Level A

Exercise 1
Jane is going to go to the supermarket. She needs a pound of ground beef, two pounds of potatoes, and a quart of orange juice. Jane also needs some onions, but she doesn't need any lettuce or tomatoes.

Exercise 2
Mark is going to go to the supermarket. He needs a dozen eggs, a pound of cheese, and some tomatoes. Mark also needs a package of cookies, but he doesn't need any cake or ice cream.

Writing Level B

Exercise 1
Mistakes:
chicken → ground beef
three pounds → two pounds
milk → orange juice
some tomatoes → some onions
onions → tomatoes

Exercise 2
Shopping List: 1 doz. eggs, 1 lb. cheese, 2 tomatoes, 1 pkg. cookies

Exercise 3
Mark is going to go to the supermarket. He needs a dozen eggs, a pound of cheese, and two tomatoes. Mark also needs some cookies, but he doesn't need any cake or ice cream.

Game: Find the Food Levels A and B

onion, bananas, eggs, hot peppers, apples, lettuce, potato, chicken

UNIT 7

Grammar Level A

Exercise 1
A: Were Marta and Pedro in the U.S. in 1985?
B: Yes, they were.

A: Was Marta a cook?
B: No, she wasn't. She was a cashier.
A: Was Pedro a cashier, too?
B: No, he wasn't. He was a delivery person.
A: Were they happy with their jobs?
B: Marta was happy, but Pedro wasn't very happy.

Exercise 2
(Answers will vary.)

Exercise 3
a. Can you read and write English? Yes, I can.
b. Can you use a cash register? Yes, I can.
c. Can you work full-time? No, I can't.
d. OK. Can you work days? No, I can't.
   But I can work nights.
e. When can you start?
   Can you start immediately?
   I can start next month.

Exercises 4 and 5
(Answers will vary.)

Grammar Level B

Exercise 1
A: I see you worked at the ABC Drugstore, Mr. Lee.
B: Were you a delivery person?
A: No, I was a cashier.
B: Was it a full-time job?
A: No, it wasn't. It was part-time. I was a full-time student then.
A: I see. Were you happy with your job at the drugstore?
B: Yes, I was. I was very happy.
A: Were they happy with you?
B: Yes, they were.
A: Why did you leave?
B: The drugstore closed, and I was laid off.

Exercise 2
a. Can you use a cash register?
b. Can you drive a car?
c. Can you read English?
d. Can you fix a refrigerator?
e. Can you work full-time?
f. Can you work in the morning?
g. Can you start a new job immediately?

Exercise 3
(Answers may vary a little.)
a. He can use a cash register, but he can't use a sewing machine.
b. He can drive a car, but he can't drive a bus.
c. He can read English, but he can't read Spanish.
d. He can't fix a refrigerator or a stove, but he can fix a TV.
e. He can't work full-time, but he can work part-time.
f. He can work the first shift and second shift, but he can't work the third shift.
g. He can't start a new job immediately, but he can start next month.

Game: Job Search Levels A and B

Exercise 1

```
H O T E L P E T O N E S A I D
A R M T E A C H E R A S P D O
M O N E T R O C L P A B L O S
C A S T J A N I T O R R A C K
A S B V O M E N W K O E N T D
S C A R P E N T E R E D Y O U
H A K E E D I M S U M C A R E
I C E A T I M A G O G E T O N
E M R I L C O O K F O O D I T
R O N L H M V K R N W T Y O N
```

Exercise 2
a. cook   b. baker   c. doctor   d. cashier
e. teacher   f. janitor   g. carpenter   h. paramedic

Writing Level A

Exercise 1
Oscar is going to apply for this job. The notice is for a full-time hospital worker. No experience is necessary. The job pays $5.25/hr. It's for the evening/second shift, and it starts immediately/now.

Exercise 2
Olga is going to apply for this job. The notice is for a part-time cashier. Experience is necessary. The job pays $6.30/hr. It's for the morning/first shift, and it starts June 1.

Writing Level B

Exercise 1
Mistakes: part-time → full-time.
            $5.75/hr. → $5.25/hr.
            day shift → evening shift/second shift
            next week → immediately/now

Exercise 2
(possible answers)
The job is for a full-time or part-time cashier. No experience is necessary. The job pays $6.24/hr. It's for all shifts, and it starts next month. You can call for an interview.

UNIT 8

Grammar Level A

Exercise 1
a. me   b. you   c. him   d. her   e. it   f. us   g. them

Exercise 2
a. it, It b. them, They c. her, She d. him, He
e. me, I f. us, We g. you, you

Exercise 3
a. Frank was at school.
b. Gina and Tony were at the movies.
c. Sandy was at work.
d. Billy and Rick were at home.

Exercise 4
A: Was Frank at home last night?
B: No, he wasn't. He was at school.
A: Where were Gina and Tony?
B: They were at the movies.
A: Were Billy and Rick at the movies, too?
B: No, they weren't.
A: Oh. Where were they?
B: They were at home.
A: Where was Sandy?
B: She was at work.

Exercise 5
a. Where were b. How many ... were c. When was
d. What was e. Who was

Grammar Level B

Exercise 1
(see Grammar Level A, Exercise 1)

Exercise 2
a. it b. It, They c. them d. He, him e. her
f. she g. She, I, you h. you, me, We

Exercise 3
a. were b. were c. was d. was e. was
f. were g. was h. was

Excercise 4
a. Where was
b. Was your grandmother born
c. What was
d. Were they
e. How long were they
f. How old was she
g. how old was your grandfather?

Writing Level A

Exercise 2
Do you have the screwdriver? I need it. Bob doesn't have it. I asked him. Anna was here, too. I also asked her. She saw it yesterday. It was on the pegboard next to the pliers. The pliers are there now. I can see them to the left of the hammer. But I can't see the screwdriver! Please call me.

Writing Level B

Exercise 1
a. it b. it c. him d. her e. She f. it
g. It h. them i. me

Exercise 2
Do you have the scissors? I need them. Bob doesn't have them. I asked him. Anna was here, too. I also asked her. She saw them yesterday. They were on the pegboard next to the pliers. The pliers are there now. I can see them to the left of the hammer. But I can't see the scissors! Please call me.

Game: Where are the nails? Levels A and B

on the floor, in the wall, in a jar, next to the hammer, on the shelf, between the gloves and the hammer, next to the paint cans/under the table, in the corner/above the saws

UNIT 9

Grammar Level A

Exercise 1
a. smaller b. big c. shorter d. fat e. older
f. longer g. thin h. younger i. taller

Exercise 2
a. Yes b. Yes c. No d. No e. No f. Yes

Exercise 3
a. Lee is older than Rob.
b. Rob is fatter than Lee.
c. Lee is shorter than Rob.
d. Lee's hair is shorter than Rob's hair.
e. Lee's jacket is smaller than Rob's jacket.

Grammar Level B

Exercise 1
a. smaller b. bigger c. longer d. shorter
e. older f. thinner g. fatter h. younger i. taller

Exercise 2
a. No, that's wrong. Mary is younger than Ann.
b. Yes, that's right.
c. Yes, that's right.
d. No, that's wrong. Mary's hair is shorter than Ann's hair.
e. That's wrong. Ann's sweater is smaller than Mary's sweater.
f. That's right.
g. That's wrong. Mary's skirt is shorter.
h. That's right.

Exercise 3
a. They're bigger.
b. This blouse is too big.
c. It's shorter.
d. These jeans are too short.
e. It's smaller.
f. These shoes are too big.

Writing Level A

Exercise 1
a. Today b. Store c. sweater d. two e. socks

Exercise 2
(possible answer)
Thank you for the birthday money. Today I went shopping at Robinson's Department Store. I bought a lot of clothes. I bought some jeans, some shoes, and a sweater. Now I have clothes for my new job/school.

Writing Level B

Exercise 1
Today → Yesterday
Robinson's → Lacy's
tools → clothes
skirt → sweater
three → two
shoes → socks

Exercise 2

2 pr. socks @ $1.25	$2.50
1 sweater	$15.35
1 jacket	$89.23
Subtotal	$107.08
Tax	$9.93
Total	$117.01

Exercise 3
(possible answer)
Thank you for the birthday money. Today I went shopping at R & S Department store. I bought a lot of clothes. I bought some socks, a striped sweater, and a black jacket. I paid $117.01. Now I have clothes for my new job. Thanks again.

Game: Word Search Levels A and B

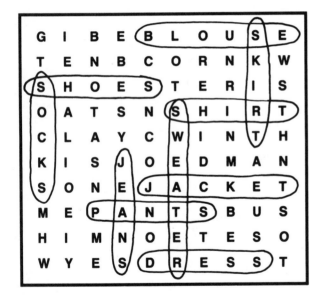

UNIT 10

Grammar Level A

Exercise 1
a. walk   b. Do...take the bus   c. Do...take
d. car, Do you...drive   e. Are

Exercise 2
a. She never walks to school.
b. She hardly ever takes the bus.
c. She sometimes takes the train.
d. She usually drives to school.
e. She's always late for school.

Grammar Level B

Exercise 1
a. ever   b. never   c. Do   d. ever   e. take   f. take
g. How   h. long   i. How   j. much   k. Are   l. ever

Exercise 2
a. He never walks to school.
b. He sometimes takes the train, but he usually takes the bus.
c. The trip is usually about twenty minutes.
d. The trip is/costs $1.25.
e. He is sometimes late for school.

Exercises 3 and 4
(Answers will vary.)

Writing Level A

Exercise 2

December 21

Dear Helen
    Hi. How are you? Do you remember my brother Ken? You met him last year. He moved in November from Yorktown, and now he lives near you in Portsmouth. I always visit him in January.
    I usually take the train to Yorktown, but this time I'm going to drive to Portsmouth. The trip is usually about two hours. I hardly ever arrive late.
    Ken has to work, and I sometimes have some free time. Are you going to be home on January 17? I can drive to your house. It's always nice to see you!
                    Please write soon.
                    Dan

Writing Level B

Exercise 2

April 6

Dear Kim,
    How are you? I think about you a lot. Today I bought a plane ticket to Allentown. I'm going to visit my brother. I always visit him in April. The ticket usually costs about $300. This time there was a special fare, and it was only $250. The trip usually takes three hours.
    My brother sometimes meets me at the airport, but this time I'm going to rent a car. The trip from the airport to my brother's apartment usually takes an hour. We are hardly ever late.
    I usually stay in Allentown for a week, but this time I'm going to be there for about a month. Can we meet one weekend? It's always nice to see you!
                    Please write.
                    Anna

Game: "T" Search Levels A and B

train, traffic, table, truck, tools, time, ten o'clock, telephone, test, tablets, tomatoes, tuna fish, tea, tissues, TV, tree, train station